Babe Ruth: The Life and Legacy of Major League Baseball Player

By Charles River Editors

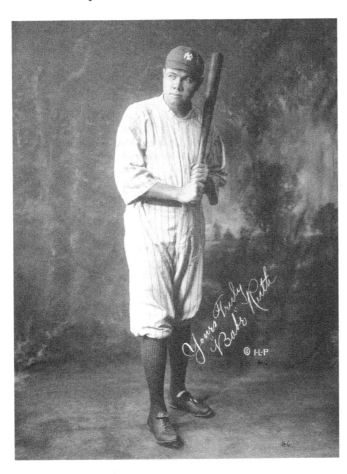

About Charles River Editors

Charles River Editors provides superior editing and original writing services across the digital publishing industry, with the expertise to create digital content for publishers across a vast range of subject matter. In addition to providing original digital content for third party publishers, we also republish civilization's greatest literary works, bringing them to new generations of readers via ebooks.

Sign up here to receive updates about free books as we publish them, and visit Our Kindle Author Page to browse today's free promotions and our most recently published Kindle titles.

Introduction

A 1914 card featuring Ruth on the Baltimore Orioles

"I only have one superstition: I make sure to touch all the bases when I hit a home run." – Babe Ruth

"I roomed with a suitcase. About the only time I saw him was at the ballpark or on a train. He couldn't come through a hotel lobby without being mobbed by fans. If he ate at the hotel, diners pestered him for autographs and his food got cold. I got to know him best on sleeper jumps. He loved to play poker. First thing he'd do on boarding the train would be to peel off his jacket and shirt and holler for a deck of cards." – Ping Bodie, one of Ruth's early teammates

As one of America's oldest and most beloved sports, baseball has long been touted as the national pastime, but of all the millions of people who have played it over the last few centuries, the first name that many associate with Major League Baseball is Babe Ruth, whose career spanned over 20 years on the way to becoming the sport's biggest legend. The Bambino came onto the scene as a pitcher for the Boston Red Sox, only to be infamously sold to the rival New York Yankees, where he went on to set records for most home runs (714), runs batted in (2,213), walks (2,062), slugging percentage (.690), and on-base plus slugging (1.164). The Sultan of Swat's records would take decades to be surpassed, but he also managed to win more than 20 games as a pitcher for Boston, along with three World Series before heading to New York. Boston wouldn't win another championship for over 80 years after Ruth's departure, a drought famously referred to as "The Curse of the Bambino."

As if he wasn't accomplished enough in Boston, Ruth went on to become a pop culture fixture in New York while playing 15 years for the Yankees on some of the sport's most legendary teams. In addition to leading the Bronx Bombers to four World Series during his time there, Ruth set several single season and career records, elevating the team and MLB itself in ways that athletes could hardly dream of today. Ruth's impact could be keenly felt in a 1922 article authored by Heywood Broun, "Cutting the Heart of the Plate," which said of him, "No one ever requires more than one glance to identify Babe Ruth. Even a wholly ignorant person who had never heard of him would probably stop in wonder at the sight of Babe waddling by. It must be clear to all beholders that here is some great, primitive force harking back to the dim days of the race. William Jennings Bryan might well look upon the Babe and recant. To be sure, a certain ingenuity was required to fit just the proper name upon this personality. As George Herman Ruth he might have gone far but he could hardly have reached the heights. The man who made him by the gift of "Babe" ought to draw a substantial royalty from Ruth's mighty income. But probably no single individual hit upon the happy thought. Undoubtably a mass movement was required. Babe Ruth has all the vigor and vitality of a piece of folk literature."

Over a century after his MLB debut, Ruth remains as well known as ever, and people continue to discuss his exploits both on and off the field. Ruth used to wink at his reputation, joking, "I learned early to drink beer, wine and whiskey. And I think I was about 5 when I first chewed tobacco." Biographer Leigh Montville described a typical scene after a game: "The outrageous life fascinated [pitcher Waite] Hoyt, the…freedom of it, the nonstop, pell-mell charge into excess. How did a man drink so much and never get drunk? ... The puzzle of Babe Ruth never was dull, no matter how many times Hoyt picked up the pieces and stared at them. After games he would follow the crowd to the Babe's suite. No matter what the town, the beer would be iced and the bottles would fill the bathtub."

Given the passage of time, people tend to debate how good Ruth would be today, including most recently a current MLB reliever, Adam Ottavino, who claimed he would strike out Ruth every time. That claim became even more controversial when Ottavino joined none other than the Yankees ahead of the 2019 season, which led to the reliever walking back some of the comments. But even as far back as 1929, Bucky Harris may have foreseen debates of this kind by pointing out, "These other home run hitters are neck and neck. When the Babe was doing his stuff, he was miles ahead of his field. A great fielder and thrower, too. A good base runner. Made the right play instinctively. And don't forget he was one of the great left-hand pitchers of his time. When was there ever another ball player like that?"

Babe Ruth: The Life and Legacy of Major League Baseball's Most Famous Player profiles how Ruth became one of the most important athletes in American history. Along with pictures of important people, places, and events, you will learn about Babe Ruth like never before.

From Pigtown to Beantown

"Brother Matthias had the right idea about training a baseball club. He made every boy on the team play every position in the game, including the bench. A kid might pitch a game one day and find himself behind the bat the next or perhaps out in the sun-field. You see Brother Matthias' idea was to fit a boy to jump in in any emergency and make good. So whatever I have at the bat or on the mound or in the outfield or even on the bases, I owe directly to Brother Matthias." – Babe Ruth

George Herman Ruth, Jr. was born on February 6, 1895, in Baltimore, Maryland, in a neighborhood known by the less than flattering name "Pigtown." A second generation Baltimorean and a third generation American, he would be one of seven children born to George and Katherine Ruth, but the only son to survive infancy, growing up with his younger sister Mamie. He was bilingual as a child, speaking both English and German, but he was sent away to St. Mary's Industrial School for Boys, a Roman Catholic boarding school and orphanage, when he was only 7 years old, likely because it was decided that living in an apartment above his father's saloon was no life for a young child. He remained at St. Mary's for 12 years, during which time he received an education in reading, writing, arithmetic. He also received vocational training as a shirt maker and carpenter.

Ruth's birthplace

A chain of events that certainly seemed to be a tragedy for young Ruth proved to be his making. Discussing one of the Xaverian Brothers that ran the school, Ruth recalled, "I think I was born as a hitter the first day I ever saw him hit a baseball. I can remember it as if it were yesterday. It was during the summer of 1902, my first year in St. Mary's. The baseball of that time was a lump of mush, and by the time St. Mary's got hold of one it was considerably less. But Brother Matthias would stand at the end of the yard, a finger mitt on his left hand and a bat is his right, toss the ball up with his left hand and give it a terrific belt with the bat he held in his right hand. When he felt like it he could hit it a little harder and make the ball clear the fence in center field. ... I would just stand there and watch him, bug-eyes."

Speaking of the special relationship Ruth shared with Matthias, biographer Robert Creamer later observed, "Ruth revered Brother Matthias ... which is remarkable, considering that Matthias was in charge of making boys behave and that Ruth was one of the great natural misbehavers of all time." Creamer added, "George Ruth caught Brother Matthias' attention early, and the calm, considerable attention the big man gave the young hellraiser from the waterfront struck a spark of response in the boy's soul ... [that may have] blunted a few of the more savage teeth in the gross man whom I have heard at least a half-dozen of his baseball contemporaries describe with admiring awe and wonder as 'an animal.'" If there was any doubt about Ruth's ability to cause mischief, he once admitted, "If it wasn't for baseball, I'd be in either the penitentiary or the cemetery."

More interested in the boy's character than his baseball prowess, Brother Mattias played Ruth in many different positions, even though he was left-handed and therefore seemed best suited for the outfield. Then, one day, when Ruth made the mistake of deriding the boy pitching for a game, Brother Matthias challenged him to do better. Ruth stepped up to the plate and proved that he indeed could pitch better than the other young man. Ruth himself would later claim, "As soon as I got out there I felt a strange relationship with the pitcher's mound. It was as if I'd been born out there. Pitching just felt like the most natural thing in the world. Striking out batters was easy."

Pictures of Ruth in 1912 at St. Mary's Industrial School for Boys in Baltimore

By the time he turned 18, Ruth had made a name for himself in the area as both a pitcher and a hitter. So remarkable was his talent that the Brothers allowed him to leave campus on the weekends to play for local teams, and brother Paul, who was the school's superintendent, would orchestrate Ruth's big break. Writing for *The Independent* magazine in 1920, journalist Sidney Reid told readers, "[F]ive years ago last winter Brother Paul notified Jack Dunn, manager of the Baltimore [Oriole]s, and Dunn came to the school and watched Ruth play ball. He was catcher on the school's first team then. Dunn took Ruth immediately and soon sent very favorable reports to Brother Paul, who was the boy's guardian. Said Dunn: 'Ruth can hit harder than anyone I ever saw and he is so strong that there are no two men in the club who can put him on his back in wrestling.' The boy was only nineteen years of age then. He has grown since. He is not only phenomenally strong, he's also phenomenally tough — speaking athletically."

DUNN, BALTIMORE

Dunn's baseball card

That was in 1914, and the Orioles were a minor league team in the International League. When Ruth left Baltimore to travel to Fayetteville, North Carolina for spring training, it marked the first time he had ever left his hometown. Ruth's young age, and the fact that Dunn kept a special eye on him, earned him his famous nickname, shortened from "Dunnie's babe," but when he made his first professional appearance on the field on March 7, 1914 in an inter-squad game, he proved that he could play baseball as well as any grown man, and better than most. The second time he came to the plate to bat, he hit a home run to right field, one that was rumored to be even longer than that hit in Fayetteville by the legendary Jim Thorpe.

Thorpe

Ruth soon went on to play in an exhibition game against the famed Philadelphia Phillies, pitching in the 4th, 5th, and 6th innings. The batters got two runs off of him in the 4th, but he held them hitless in the 5th and 6th innings. In this and the games that followed, Ruth made it clear that he would allow few batters to hit any ball he pitched. Likewise, when he began playing regular season ball, he demonstrated that he was as formidable at the plate as he was at the mound.

In spite of his prowess, the Orioles remained largely ignored by both the press and the fans, and as the team continued to lose money, Dunn considered moving the team to Richmond, Virginia, or even selling a minority interest in the club. Ultimately, both these possibilities failed to materialize, and Dunn had to sell off some of his best players. Though a rookie, Ruth went to the Boston Red Sox, joining the team on July 11, 1914. According to Sidney Reid, "The Red Sox used him as a pitcher. … He played two seasons with the Red Sox and helped them to win a world's championship series. … Ruth did good pitching for the Red Sox. He didn't know that the Athletics were invincible so he went ahead and beat them. But his ability to knock home runs and bring other runners across the plate with him made him too valuable to use as a pitcher who of necessity would have to rest two-thirds of the time. So the Red Sox put him at first base and he came to bat every day they played. And he did things in home run getting that had never been done before." Indeed, Ruth was so good at pitching that Del Baker, who played and coached in MLB for decades, told one of his teammates that Ruth "had real good stuff. I mean real good. His fast ball took off and his curve was quick. And he could get the ball over. He was always around the plate. It was funny, though. He had a cute trick of sticking out his tongue on a curve ball. But even though you knew it was coming, you had trouble hitting it. I caught him once in California in an exhibition game one fall. He still had something left. I remember we beat the other team managed by Ty Cobb, 8-7, and Ty sure hated to lose."

A picture of Ruth pitching for the Red Sox

Baker

Shortly after heading to the Red Sox, Ruth met and courted Helen Woodford, a 16-year-old waitress, and the two teenagers married on October 17, 1914, at St. Paul's Catholic Church in Ellicott City, Maryland. Sadly, life was moving too fast for a young man who grew up in an orphanage to keep up, and constant travel presented many challenges for their marriage, leading Ruth to begin a pattern of serial adultery that would last for the rest of his life. It did not help that the two could not have children, and that the infant girl they adopted in 1921 may have been Ruth's illegitimate daughter by his mistress, Juanita Jennings. Helen left Ruth in 1925 and eventually moved to Watertown, Massachusetts, where she lived with a dentist named Edward Kinder. Though the two never married, she referred to herself as "Mrs. Kinder" until her death in a house fire in January 1929.

Ruth and his wife

The Red Sox

After his marriage, Ruth began his career as a major league ballplayer, reporting to Hot Springs, Arkansas in March 1915 for spring training. Since the Red Sox already had two excellent left-handed pitchers in Dutch Leonard and Ray Collins, Ruth was not part of the team's starting pitching rotation, and when he did start, Ruth did not impress. In his first start, he took the loss in the third game of the season, but injuries among Boston's starting pitchers, along with ineffective pitching, gave Ruth another chance. After Ruth performed well as a reliever, manager Bill Carrigan put Ruth in as a starting pitcher, and the Sox won a rain-shortened seven inning game.

Leonard (left) and Carrigan

10 days later, Carrigan had Ruth start against the New York Yankees. After taking a 3-2 lead into the 9th inning, Ruth lost the game 4-3 in 13 innings, but in the process, Ruth established his true place in baseball as a power hitter. Hitting ninth in the rotation, Ruth launched a massive home run off of Yankee's pitcher Jack Warhop into the upper deck of the Polo Grounds in right field. The shot awed the crowd because home runs were a rarity in baseball at the time. Winning the game, Warhop would retire from major league baseball in August 1915 after an undistinguished eight-season career. Today, he is best known for being the first major league pitcher to give up a home run to Babe Ruth.

Satisfied with Ruth's pitching, Carrigan gave him a spot in the Red Sox's starting rotation, and he finished the season with a record of 18-8 as a pitcher. His hitting statistics were also impressive, with Ruth batting .315 with four home runs. The Red Sox won the American League pennant, but with the pitching staff healthy by the end of the season, Ruth did not pitch in the 1915 World Series. Boston won the series in five games against the National League champion Philadelphia Phillies. Ruth pinch-hit in Game 5 and grounded out.

For all of his success as a pitcher, however, Ruth was beginning to make a name for himself as a hitter. He was gaining a reputation for long home runs - in once such instance, during a game at Sportsman's Park against the St. Louis Browns, Ruth's home run hit soared over Grand Avenue and broke the window of a Chevrolet dealership.

During the 1916 season, the attention of the baseball world focused on Ruth's pitching. He had several pitching duels with Washington Senators pitcher Walter Johnson, and in their five meetings during the season, Ruth won four of them. Two of Ruth's victories were by the score of 1-0, including one in a 13 inning game. Of the shutout that did not go into extra innings, American League President Ban Johnson said, "That was one of the best ball games I have ever seen." For the entire season, Ruth led the league with a 1.75 ERA and nine shutouts on his way to a record of 23-12, and his nine shutouts set a record for a left-hander that would not be eclipsed until 1978.

Boston won the pennant again and went on to beat the Brooklyn Robins (later the Brooklyn Dodgers) in the World Series in five games. Unlike in 1915, Ruth started Game 2, which he won 2-1 in 14 innings, the longest World Series game until 2005. Ruth's performance remains the longest postseason complete game victory.

A picture of Ruth during batting practice in 1916

After the 1916 season, Carrigan retired as the Red Sox's player/manager. Throughout his career, Ruth, who played for four managers currently in the National Baseball Hall of Fame, maintained that Carrigan (who is not enshrined) was the best manager he ever had.

In addition to losing its manager, the Red Sox also underwent other changes during that offseason. The team was purchased by a three-man group headed by New York theatrical promoter Harry Frazee, and Jack Barry was hired to manage the team.

Frazee

The 1917 season was an exemplary one for Ruth personally. He finished the season with a record of 24-13, a 2.01 ERA, and six shutouts, but he was not used much as a batter, despite hitting .325 with two home runs. The team as a whole was not so fortunate, finishing second in the league and nine games behind the Chicago White Sox.

One of Ruth's more memorable starts of the season occurred against the Washington Senators on June 24. After the home plate umpire Brick Owens called his first four pitches as balls, Ruth charged home from the mound and threw a punch at him. Owens ejected Ruth from the game, and American League President Ban Johnson later suspended him for a week and fined him $100. The Philadelphia *Evening Public Ledger* complained, "Far be It from us to wish any guy bad luck, but It appears that Babe Ruth escaped too easily after his fight with Umpire Owens on the ball field. Ban Johnson dismissed the matter with a fine of $100 and a suspension of one week. This does not seem enough, and It Is certain that a player of less importance would have been treated rather harshly. Ruth is one of the stars of the league and a prolonged absence would have ruined Boston's pennant chances. Also the gate receipts would have suffered. So Battling Ban became as meek as a lamb and decided to 'give the boy another chance.'"

Johnson

America's entry into World War I on April 6, 1917 affected the sport of baseball as it did other parts of American life. Most baseball players in MLB became subject to the draft when it was introduced in September of that year, including Red Sox manager Jack Barry, who was called up after the 1917 season. To replace him, Frazee hired the president of the International League, Ed Barrow, who had 30 years of experience in baseball, but had never played the game. With much of the team gone with the Army, Barrow had a lot of holes to fill in the starting lineup. Ruth noticed these vacancies himself, and he lobbied Barrow to be allowed to play different positions when he was not starting as pitcher. During the 1918 exhibition season, Barrow used Ruth at first base and in the outfield, but he restricted him to pitching as the season opener drew near.

Barrow

When the 1918 season began, Barrow followed the advice of Red Sox player Harry Hooper and played Ruth at other positions when he was not scheduled to pitch. Hooper pointed out that the crowds were larger on the days Ruth played, primarily because they wanted to see if Ruth would crush another huge home run. After Ruth began to be played more frequently, Ruth hit four home runs in four consecutive games, and for the first time in his career, Ruth was placed higher in the batting order than ninth. Ruth wound up being used primarily as an outfielder in the war-shortened season, and he hit .300 with 11 home runs, earning him a share of the MLB home run crown with Tilly Walker of the Philadelphia Athletics. In his occasional outings as a pitcher, he compiled a 13-7 record with a 2.22 ERA.

Hooper

The Red Sox, behind Ruth's hitting, won their third American League pennant in four years and faced the Chicago Cubs in the World Series. Ruth pitched in Game 1, winning it for the Red Sox in a 1-0 shutout. The *New York Tribune* reported, "In a wonderful pitching duel, in which each manager staked his most formidable southpaw, the mighty 'Babe' Ruth vanquished the giant [Chicago Cubs pitcher Hippo] Vaughn by a score of 1 to 0. Though beaten, neither Vaughn nor the supporting Cub cast was in any way disgraced. It was such a game as one seldom sees in the final title battles, something which approached the acme of perfection in every line. As had been predicted, this one game at least made good the prophecy that sterling box work would predominate. Perhaps because of the excellence of the rival pitchers the hard fought engagement did not develop the customary thrills one looks for in the blue ribbon of sports. The game was just a bit too perfect to be as interesting as it might. There were no errors, either of commission or omission. There were wonderful fielding plays, it is true, but these were the exception rather than the rule, and they were, turned with a daring that made them appear scarcely part of mechanical, machine-like precision." Hitting ninth as pitcher, Ruth had no hits in three at bats.

Before Game 4, Ruth injured his pitching hand in a fight, but he started the game anyway. The results were not stellar, as he gave up seven hits and six walks, but the team's fielding and his own batting efforts (including a 4th inning triple) led to a 2-0 Red Sox lead. The Cubs tied the game in the 8th inning, but the Red Sox answered to take the lead 3-2 going into the 9th. Ruth was relieved on the mound after giving up a hit and a walk to start the last inning, but he was sent to play left field so he would stay in the batting order. Reliever Joe Bush retired the remaining Cubs pitchers to give Ruth his second win of the World Series, and his third and last World Series pitching victory. Before giving up a run in Game 4, Ruth had pitched 28 2/3 consecutive scoreless innings, a record for the World Series that was only broken in 1961 by New York Yankees pitcher Whitey Ford.

At the end of the war-shortened 1918 season, Ruth faced the possibility of being drafted into the Army. He managed to avoid this by taking a job in a Pennsylvania steel mill, where he was hired mostly because of his ability to play on the mill's baseball team. Upon the end of the war that November, the threat of conscription was lifted and Ruth was able to prepare for the 1919 season. It would prove to be a pivotal season in his career.

Among other things, the 1919 season was the last season Ruth would be used primarily as a pitcher. In fact, he only pitched in 17 out of 130 games, with an 8-5 record. Barrow only used him in the pitching rotation early in the season, when the manager hoped for a second consecutive pennant. As it became clear that was not going to happen, Barrow moved him to other positions that allowed Ruth to concentrate on the kind of hitting that drew crowds. He hit a home run against the Yankees on Opening Day, and another one during a month-long batting slump. After he was no longer a pitcher, however, Ruth went on a home run spree, which drew widespread public and private attention. Journalist Sidney Reid noted, "During April of last year he made one home run, during May two, during June four, July nine, August seven, September six. Only nine of these homers were made in Boston; the others while he was on the road. …he got at least three home runs at the expense of every opposing club. From the Detroit pitchers he got seven home runs. But there was an exception — Washington. He got no home run from Washington till the very end of the season."

1919 was a record season for the slugger. By mid-July, Ruth had hit 11 home runs, tying the number from 1918. On July 29, Ruth hit his 16th homer, which tied the American League single season mark set by Ralph "Socks" Seybold in 1902, and on September 8, he tied the Major League record of 24 set by Buck Freeman in 1899.

As the attention of the baseball world focused on Ruth's feats, people wondered what other records he could aim for that season. Sportswriters scouring the records found that Ned Williamson of the 1884 Chicago White Stockings had hit 27 home runs in that season, and Ruth tied that on September 20, during "Babe Ruth Day" at Fenway Park, hitting a game-winning home run in the bottom of the ninth. Four days later, he hit his 28th homer against the Yankees to break the record, a feat that even the partisan *New York Herald* described in awe-struck terms: "The first ball was high and wide, and Ruth let it go by with a scowl. The second one was a slow curved ball, and it drifted by the port side of the young giant about waist high. Every ounce of the huge frame went into the swing. He met the ball fairly, and it shot toward the roof of the grandstand with such speed that few could follow its course. It cleared the roof, and Ruth started to trot around the bases. High on the corner of the roof a boy who had gone up to furl the flags, waved his hands excitedly to indicate that the ball had gone out of the stadium into the lot next door. The announcer ran down the field to verify this by word of mouth. Some years back Shoeless Joe Jackson held the record for long hits at the Polo Grounds. His hit landed in the space between the left field stands and the bleachers. Ruth's hit went fairly out of the grounds, the first time that a ball has been driven out of the place since it was built. There is no way of measuring the exact distance of the hit, but the writer is willing to believe that it is the longest distance ever covered by a batted ball."

Ruth hit another against the Washington Senators to end the season with 29 home runs, but in spite of his phenomenal hitting prowess, the Red Sox finished the season in sixth place, 20 ½ games behind the Chicago White Sox.

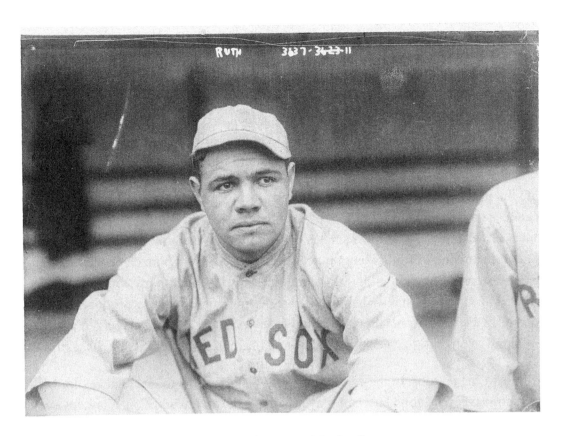

Pictures of Ruth with the Sox

A Bronx Bomber

Thanks to his record-setting season, Babe Ruth had become the most popular player in baseball. Attendance for 1919 broke all records in Boston and at every ballpark around the country. So valuable a player was Ruth for the Red Sox that he reportedly signed a 3-year contract to play for the team in March 1919. At $10,000 a year, Ruth would be one of the highest paid players in baseball, but Ruth, fully aware of his value, reportedly demanded that his contract be renegotiated. He was quoted in *The Boston Globe* in October 1919 as saying, "You can say for me that I will not play with the Red Sox unless I get $20,000. You may think that sounds like a pipe dream, but it is the truth. I feel that I made a bad move last year when I signed a three years' contract to play for $30,000. The Boston club realized much on my value and I think I am entitled to twice as much as my contract calls for. The contract has two years to run, I know. It may be ironbound as far as the Boston club is concerned, but I think with the 10-day clause in it I am entitled to the same privileges as the club. Well, that is a matter for the owners to right, and as my business is in another direction just at present I am going to wait to hear from them."

With Ruth threatening to sit out the season or cash in on his popularity in other ways, Louis Dougher of the *Washington Times* reported, "Though has two more years to complete his contract with the Boston Red Sox at a salary of $10,000 yearly. Ruth would sign a new one calling for $20,000 yearly. Furthermore, he says he will not play with the Boston club unless his wishes are granted. Last spring Ruth held out until the last minute. He wanted a salary of $15,000, if our memory be correct, but finally compromised by signing a three-year-contract calling for a salary of $10,000 yearly. All that took place before he began hammering home runs until he had taken ail previous big league records for this stunt. He admitted that he was satisfied with the treatment given him by both Harry Frazee and Ed Barrow. He proved it by playing fine ball all season. But Babe has listened to serpent tongues. Now he would quit playing ball unless the Boston club agrees to make a new contract calling for $20,000 a year."

Despite the ultimatum, it was still quite a shock when Frazee sold Ruth's contract to the New York Yankees on December 26, 1919. Why exactly Frazee sold Ruth's contract is not entirely clear, but what is known is that the Yankees wanted to bring Ruth on board to improve their team. According to one of Ruth's biographers, Jim Reisler, "Why Frazee needed cash in 1919— and large infusions of it quickly—is still, more than 80 years later, a mystery." That said, it's known that Frazee was constantly in need of cash to fund his Broadway productions, and Ruth's salary demands also put financial pressure on Frazee, as it led to other players to ask for more money. On top of all that, Frazee still owed as much as $125,000 for the purchase of the club.

Regardless of the reasons, in the end, Frazee sold Ruth's rights to the Yankees for $100,000, the largest sum ever paid for a baseball player at the time, and in addition, Yankees owner Jacob Ruppert lent Frazee $350,000 secured by a mortgage on Fenway Park. The transaction was contingent on Ruth signing a new contract, which he agreed to. Under the terms, he was to fulfill the remaining two years of his contract, but he would also be given a $20,000 bonus payable over the next two seasons.

Ruppert

The deal was announced on January 6, 1920, and in announcing the deal, the *Washington Herald* commented that the "sale of Ruth not only elevates the trading of baseball players to inclusion in the category of sugar, shoes, clothing and other high-priced necessities, but records a sale at more than double the highest price heretofore paid for a player."

The *Associated Press* reported, "The acquisition of Ruth strengthens the Yankee club in its weakest department. With the added hitting power of Ruth, Bob Shawkey, one of the Yankee pitchers, said yesterday the New York club should be a pennant winner next season. For several seasons the Yankees have been experimenting with outfielders, but never have been able to land a consistent hitter. The short right field wall at the Polo Grounds should prove an easy target for Ruth next season and, playing seventy- seven games at home, it would not be surprising if Ruth surpassed his home-run record of twenty-nine circuit clouts next summer."

According to Marty Appel in his history of the Yankees, "This was the biggest deal in baseball history. It changed the fortunes of two high-profile franchises for decades/ Babe Ruth would take baseball soaring into a new era as the number-one game is the Golden Age of Sports. It is always difficult to say any athlete is bigger than the game. But Babe Ruth may have qualified…He certainly became an overnight celebrity when he came to New York, and may have been the best-known American after the president throughout the remained of his career. Many European immigrants first became away of baseball by his presence---his easy to remember name, his easily identified look, his love of celebrity. If they could talk about Baby Ruth and smile when his name was mentioned, they were on the road to assimilation. He looked different. His moon face with the boyish grin, atop a barrel chest and skinny legs, made him easy to pick out in any group photo. He wasn't fat but was rather top-heavy, and not until late in his career did he occasionally let himself get out of shape. He could run the bases well and cover a lot of ground in the outfield: Otherwise, Barrow might have converted him into a first baseman. And he was loveable. Even when he'd get himself into a tight spot, he'd win over the fans with a humble apology, like a child scolded and sent to his room. He had a gift for saying the right things in interviews and being the all-American boy for kids even if he really wasn't."

Ruth with the Yankees in 1920

The Polo Grounds in the 1920s

Ruth began his career with the Yankees in the 1920 season somewhat ignominiously. By the end of April, the Yankees were 4-7 (the Red Sox led the American League at 10-2) and Ruth had done little due to an injury. The *New York Tribune* told readers late in April, "The Yanks, with the most formidable batting array and a pitching staff that reads invincible, have been through the same trouble as the Giants. They have not been able to get started. Babe Ruth, the $150,000 slugger, has not slugged at any place to date and very young or very worn-out pitchers have been laughing into their flannel sleeves at the Yanks...They lost the very first game of the season to the Athletics; then they won just one. After this they went to Boston, where they made the Red Sox look like a baseball team and caused the Boston fans to wonder why Babe Ruth brought all that money in the baseball market."

On May 1, however, things began to change. Playing for the first time in the Polo Grounds against his old team, Ruth hit a home run completely out of the park. This sparked the Yankees to a 6-0 shutout over the Red Sox, and New York went on to take three of four games in the series. W. O. McGeehan of the *New York Tribune* described the Bambino's blast: Babe Ruth hit a home run that cleared the top of the right field Stands by thirty feet at the Polo Grounds yesterday. All of which would tend to indicate that the Yankees, after leading a life of shame since the start of the season, were about to hit the straight and narrow trail that leads pennantward. Judges of distance declare that the Ruthian swat of yesterday traveled much more rapidly than his twenty-eighth homer of last season, which also cleared the roof. It was the first homer for the "Babe" this season, which is somewhat reassuring, In view of the fact that the morbid-minded were inclined to believe that the "Babe" might have lost his wallop after the injuries he received on opening day, It was the first ball pitched In the sixth that Ruth sent out of the lot. This being the first game the Yanks have wrested from the Sox this season, it begins to look as though the spell of tough luck has been spiked, and the Yanks, who have been looking like an expensive pile of junk to date, are beginning to assemble themselves into a ball-playing machine."

That started a record run for Ruth. He hit his second homer on May 2, and by the end of the month he had hit a then major league record of 11 home runs. In June, he broke his own record by hitting 13 home runs. The homers kept coming through the summer, with Ruth having hit a total of 37 by the end of July. On September 4, he tied and broke the organized baseball record for home runs in a season when he snapped Perry Werden's 1885 mark of 44 in the Western League.

With each home run, Ruth's national popularity grew, and he was rapidly becoming a true folk hero, the biggest celebrity of early 1920s America. McGeehan wrote of Ruth in lyrical terms in a front page story for the *New York Tribune*, "IF the late lamented Shakespeare were a baseball writer he might use a line that he rested upon some more or less obscure hero of antiquity and say of 'Babe' Ruth, 'He doth bestride the narrow baseball fields like a Colossus.' For 'Babe' Ruth is Hercules and Thor reincarnated, the Colossus of Swat. His bat is the club of Hercules and the hammer of Thor, the symbol of sheer, primitive might before which the puny folk bow and offer worship. ... The 'Babe' was Fortune's darling, though Fortune concealed her great and kindly intentions as far as he was concerned when the 'Babe' was a boy. For the 'Babe' was born a left-hander!. Hercules was a right-hander. Thor never was pictured as wielding his hammer from the port side. None of the heroes of antiquity, as far as can be ascertained, was a southpaw."

Ruth's feats inspired the entire Yankees team, at least early on. They battled for the league lead in the early summer, but they slumped in August in the midst of the battle for the American League pennant with Chicago and Cleveland. The pennant was eventually won by Cleveland, who faced the Chicago White Sox in the 1920 World Series, which was marred by the Black Sox Scandal that came the year before. Cleveland won the Series, and while the Yankees finished third, Ruth's acquisition proved lucrative to the team as his heroics drew 1.2 million fans to the Polo Grounds, the first time any team in MLB had drawn over a million fans. All of baseball benefited, as Ruth's appearances led to the league selling 600,000 more tickets than the year before. Ruth finished his first year with the Yankees with 54 home runs, 158 runs, and 137 RBIs.

Ruth and Shoeless Joe Jackson in 1920

   By the end of his first season, it was clear Ruth would be playing in the outfield regularly, and given his stature, it is perhaps not surprising that some major leaguers couldn't believe how effective Ruth was in the field. Rip Collins, who pitched for both the Red Sox and Yankees in the early 20th century, explained, "Ruth studied opposing hitters, and he studied his own pitchers. He knew how and where every batter could be expected to hit any particular pitch. Consequently, he did a great job of playing the hitter. Many a time on the Detroit or St. Louis bench, I've seen Ruth pull down a hard-hit ball and hear the batter come back to the dugout muttering: 'What was that big slob doing playing me there?' The Babe had just played him smart, that's all—moved over a couple of steps according to the pitch, and according to his judgment as to how far, how hard, and whence that batter could be expected to hit that pitch. Ruth never made mistakes in the field. He always threw to the right base, and he had a fine arm—not like Speaker or Meusel, but you couldn't take chances against him."

Of course, people remained fixated on the long balls, and Ruth remained coy about his ability to hit homers. When asked about the key to success in 1920, he responded, "I always swing at the ball with all my might. I hit or miss big and when I miss I know it long before the umpire calls a strike on me, for every muscle in my back, shoulders and arms is groaning, 'You missed it.' And believe me, it is no fun to miss a ball that hard. Once I put myself out of the game for a few days by a miss like that." On another occasion, he merely said, "All I can tell them is pick a good one and sock it. I get back to the dugout and they ask me what it was I hit and I tell them I don't know except it looked good."

Ruth's 1921 season picked up where the 1920 season left off. On July 18, 1921, in a game against the Detroit Tigers in Detroit, he broke Roger Connor's mark for home runs in a career, 138, that had stood since Connor's retirement in 1897. On September 15, Ruth hit his 55th home run of the season, eclipsing his own single season record. *The New York Tribune* reported, "Twenty-eight thousand fans went into hysterics yesterday afternoon at the Polo Grounds, while Babe Ruth, the Swattingest Swatter of Swatdom, danced around the bases with his record breaking home run labeled "Fifty- five." It was in the first game of a double bill with the St. Louis Browns when the mighty smash came, and even the fact that the Yanks by scoring a twin victory managed to cling to the lead in the pennant race faded into insignificance beside the personal triumph of George Herman Ruth. The ball Babe hit traveled into the upper tier of the right field stand. The scores of the two games were 10 to 6 and 13 to 5, the Yanks shaking off their batting lethargy to the extent of fourteen safeties in each game."

CONNOR.—FIRST BASE.
SMOKE AND CHEW
"YUM YUM" TOBACCO.
A. BECK & CO., CHICAGO, ILL.

Connor

The Yankees clinched the American League pennant in late September, with Ruth finishing the regular season with 59 home runs, batting .378 and a slugging percentage of .846. The Yankees faced the New York Giants in the World Series in 1921, with all the games played at the Polo Grounds since it was owned by the Giants and leased by the Yankees. With Ruth in the lineup, the Yankees won the first two games. *The New York Herald* described Ruth's first game (won by the Yankees 3-0) as "spotty," and he had no home runs. During Game 2, he badly scraped his elbow while sliding into third base, and the team physician told him to sit out the rest of the series, advice that Ruth ignored. He played in the next three games and pinch-hit in Game 8, but the Yankees lost the series to the Giants, five games to three. Ruth's stats were good, but not spectacular, hitting .316 with five RBIs and his first World Series home run.

After the World Series, Ruth went on a barnstorming tour across the Northeast with teammates Bob Meusel and Bill Piercy, and in doing so, he crossed the powerful (some would say dictatorial) Commissioner Judge Kenesaw Mountain Landis. There was a rule then in force that prohibited World Series participants from playing in exhibition games in the offseason. *The Great Falls Tribune* explained, "Ruth was fined for his world's series prize, amounting to $3,362.26, and suspended until May 20 of the 1922 season by Judge Landis, commissioner of baseball, for participating in exhibition games following the close of the world's series game between the Giants and the Yankees...The suspension of Ruth for at least the first month of the American league pennant race practically means, baseball observers pointed out, that the New York slugger will have little chance of breaking his home run record of 59 next season. The decision punishing Ruth and the other players, which, in the baseball world, rests as the most important Judge Landis has made since he became commissioner, was made after two months' deliberation...Judge Landis, in his decision, said the offending players 'willfully and defiantly' violated the rules and that the situation' involved not merely rule violation 'but rather a mutinous defiance intended by the players to present this question: 'Which is the bigger. baseball or any individual in baseball?'"

Landis

   Ruth remained defiant, asserting, "I am going through with my barnstorming tour to the end. Bob Meusel and the other Yanks on my club agree with me that it will not hurt the game, as Landis fears. In fact, if anything, it will create more interest in next year's campaign for me to play out this tour. If Landis wants to put me out of organized baseball, let him do so. I will continue the tour."

A picture of Ruth in the stands on Opening Day

This was bad enough, but it was not the only problem Ruth faced going into the 1922 season. In addition to his skills as a baseball player, Ruth was becoming notorious for antics away from the diamond, and due to his fame, his every move was reported, including the bad ones. Ruth's heavy drinking and carousing was widely reported by the scandal-hungry press, and he was also clearly out of shape, but in spite of everything, on March 6, 1922, Ruth signed a new contract with the Yankees for three years at $52,000 a year, the largest sum ever paid to a baseball player at the time. Some at the time criticized such an astronomical sum being paid to a grown man to play a game. The *Bismark Tribune*, however, answered the critics: "Critics of 'Babe' Ruth's salary should not forget that they are living in America. This is a free land and it offers opportunity for advancement to every citizen. What better proof is needed than these very facts about 'Babe' Ruth. An orphan, with no parents to guide his steps and yet with all his handicaps he is raised to the seats of the mighty,' with a salary that exceeds those of the mighty. It cannot be luck. Ruth has specialized. He has trained. He has made himself the baseball swat king of America. His name is known from j coast to coast. His admirers are legion. America cannot cry down the salary 'Babe' Ruth gets. His work is measured by his followers, and it is the people who indirectly pay him. He is the best in his field. America offers similar opportunities in every line to every citizen, and should not be afraid to boast of it."

In spite of his suspension, Ruth was named the Yankees' on-field captain, working out with the team in the morning and playing exhibition games on their off days, but in his return on May 20, Ruth went 0 for 4 and was booed by the assembled crowd. On May 25, he was ejected from the game for throwing dust in the umpire's face and climbing into the stands to confront a heckler. When asked about the incident after the game, he replied, "I didn't mean to hit the umpire with the dirt, but I did mean to hit that bastard in the stands." He later elaborated, "They can boo and hoot me all they want. That doesn't matter to me. But when a fan calls insulting names from the grandstand and becomes abusive I don't intend to stand for it. This fellow today, whoever he was, called me a low-down bum and other names that got me mad, and when I went after him he ran. Furthermore, I didn't throw any dust in Hildebrand's face. It didn't go into his face, only on his sleeve. I don't know what they will do to me for this. Maybe I'll be fined or suspended for kicking on the decision, but I don't see why I should get any punishment at all. I would go into the stands again if I had to." For his actions, Ban Johnson ordered Ruth fined, suspended, and stripped of the position as team captain.

That season, which was arguably his worst to that point, Ruth only appeared in 110 games, batted .315, hit 35 home runs, and drove in 99 runs, but the Yankees won the American League pennant and faced the Giants in the World Series, only to lose 4-0-1, with Ruth only having two hits in 17 at bats. So poor was Ruth's performance in the season that many began to wonder if his best years were behind him - one sportswriter even called him an "exploded phenomenon."

The Yankees knew drastic measures had to be taken. They had invested $52,000 a year for the next three years in arguably the greatest player of his generation (or perhaps all-time), and they had no intention of seeing their investment evaporate because of Ruth's carousing and drinking. In a first. New York Yankees owner Jake Ruppert forced Ruth to sign a contract addendum with a morals clause on November 11, 1922 that stated, "It is understood and agreed by and between the parties hereto that the regulation above set forth, numbered '2' shall be construed to mean among other things, that the player shall at all times during the term of this contract and throughout the years 1922, 1923 and 1924, and the years 1925 and 1926 if this contract is renewed for such years, refrain and abstain entirely from the use of intoxicating liquors and that he shall not during the training and playing season in each year stay up later than 1 o'clock A.M. on any day without the permission and consent of the Club's manager, and it is understood and agreed that if at any time during the period of this contract, whether in the playing season or not, the player shall indulge in intoxicating liquors or be guilty of any action or misbehavior which may render him unfit to perform the services to be performed by him hereunder, the Club may cancel and terminate this contract and retain as the property of the Club, any sums of money withheld from the player's salary as above provided."

Notably, the clause excluded any mention of marital fidelity, as Ruth reportedly told Ruppert, "I'll promise to go easier on drinking and to get to bed earlier, but not for you, fifty thousand dollars, or two hundred and fifty thousand dollars will I give up women. They're too much fun."

With that exception in hand, Ruth was as good as his word, and he reported to spring training weighing only 210 pounds, the best shape of his career.

It was not only Ruth's physical condition that changed prior to the 1923 season. The Yankees began play in a new stadium in the Bronx, aptly named Yankee Stadium, and in the opening game on April 18, 1923, Ruth hit the first home run in what became known as "The House that Ruth Built." Indeed, the stadium was built with Ruth in mind; the right field fence was closer than usual to home, making it easier for a lefty to hit home runs.

A picture of Opening Day at Yankee Stadium

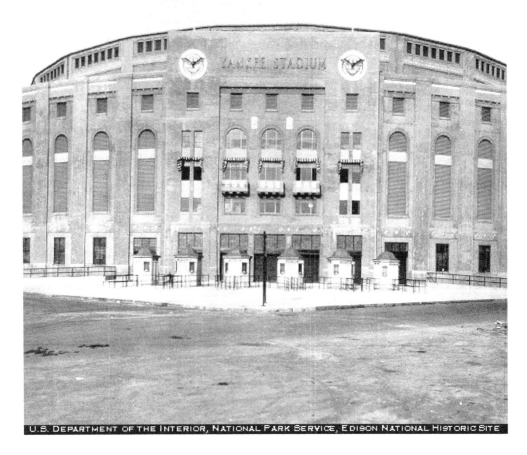

A picture of the stadium's main entrance in the 1920s

   In their newly built stadium, the Yankees flourished, dominating the American League and winning the pennant by 17 games. Ruth had a career high batting average of .393 to go with 41 home runs and 45 doubles. Facing the Giants in the World Series for the third straight year, Ruth dominated, batting .368, scoring eight runs, and hitting three home runs while leading the Yankees to their first World Series.

   In 1924, the Yankees were plagued by injuries in their quest for a fourth consecutive pennant, and even though they won 18 of 22 games in September, the Washington Senators won the American League pennant by two games. Though it was a lackluster season overall, there was a notable incident in July involving Ruth. According to historian Michael Beschloss, in July 1924, the Yankees "were in Griffith Stadium, playing a doubleheader against the Senators. In the fourth inning…the home team's Joe Judge swung his bat; the ball sailed just over the right-field line, heading toward the bleachers in foul territory. Racing to make the catch, Babe Ruth slammed into a concrete wall and was knocked unconscious. … As he lay unconscious on the field, the Yankees' trainer, Doc Woods, rushed to him with a first-aid kit and poured icy water onto his face…Ruth was out for five anxiety-producing minutes. … When the Babe finally opened his eyes, the Yankees' manager, Miller Huggins, offered to take him out, but Ruth would not hear of it. … Ruth went back into the game, showing a conspicuous limp (he had damaged his left hip) as he recorded two more hits, drawing louder cheers than usual, for his fortitude, as he rounded the bases. He even kept playing through the second game."

A picture of Ruth laying unconscious after the incident

That year, Ruth still managed to hit .378 for his only American League batting title, hitting a league-leading 46 home runs.

Ruth had kept up his efforts to stay in shape in 1923 and 1924, but by early 1925 he weighed nearly 260 pounds, and it led to a health scare that to this day is shrouded in mystery. According to journalist Bill Ballew, "Ruth…had not been feeling well since he celebrated his 30th birthday on February 6, 1925. His weight had increased significantly over the past few years, topped off by an eating and drinking binge since the end of the 1924 campaign that left Ruth tipping the scales at a robust 255 pounds. In an effort to drop some weight, Ruth reported to Hot Springs, Arkansas, in February for a combination of exercise and steam baths. His girth-reducing efforts proved fruitless before he caught the flu just prior to heading for spring training in St. Petersburg, Florida. Ruth battled his health for most of March until the team ventured north at the end of the month. On the way to Atlanta, Ruth complained of chills and fever. He continued to fight through his conditions in Chattanooga, yet thrilled the locals with two home runs after feeling too sick to take batting practice. Ruth added another roundtripper in Knoxville, only to suffer stomach cramps with a high fever shortly after the contest…The bumpy ride along the winding tracks through the Great Smoky Mountains did little to improve Ruth's condition. …several of his Yankee teammates reportedly felt nauseous on the trip prior to pulling into the Asheville train station on Depot Street. Ruth staggered off the train in front of a large crowd that had gathered to meet him and immediately fainted…Ruth was carried to a taxi by his teammates and driven to the Battery Park Hotel. He remained at the hotel overnight in the care of Dr. A.S. Jordan prior to departing the next afternoon, at 3:50. With little information to report, rumors started to circulate, including one that stated Ruth had died in Western North Carolina."

W.O. McGeehan, a sportswriter for the *New York Tribune*, named the incident "The bellyache heard 'round the world." However, as Ballew observed, "Shortly after his arrival at New York's St. Vincent's Hospital on West Eleventh Street, the Babe underwent surgery for what was described as an 'intestinal abscess.' He wound up spending seven weeks in the hospital, from April 9 through May 25. Amazingly, Ruth took the field shortly thereafter, playing in his first game on June 1. Legend says that Ruth's primary ailment was acute indigestion, caused by consuming too many hot dogs, soda pop and beer on the train ride between Knoxville and Asheville. … those close to the situation, including Yankees general manager Ed Barrow, said privately that it was a bad case of venereal disease."

Playing just 98 games, Ruth had his worst season as a Yankee; he finished with a .290 average and 25 home runs. The Yankees finished next to last in the league with a 69–85 record, their last season with a losing record until 1965.

After the horrible 1925 season, Ruth spent the offseason working out to get back into shape, and 1926 saw him return to form. He batted .372 with 47 home runs and 146 RBIs, and the Yankees won the American League Pennant and faced the St. Louis Cardinals in the World Series. The Yankees won Game 1, but the Cardinals took the next two games. In Game 4, Ruth's bat served the team well, belting three home runs and setting a record for a World Series game. The Yankees won that game and Game 5, but St. Louis took Game 6.

On the back of the pitching of Gover Cleveland Alexander, the Cardinals won Game 7 and the series, overcoming Ruth's home run in that game. He walked in the 9th inning and was thrown out trying to steal second in what many considered a blunder.

Although the Yankees lost, the 1926 World Series is indelibly part of the Ruth legend because Babe promised Johnny Sylvester, an 11-year-old boy in the hospital due to a fall from a horse, that he would hit a home run for him. Ruth later visited the boy in the hospital, and when the press learned about it, they greatly inflated it into Ruth saving the boy's life through hitting the home run.

The 1927 New York Yankees are considered one of the greatest baseball teams ever to take the field, and over 90 years later they remain known as "Murderers' Row." Featuring seven eventual Hall of Famers, the team clinched first place on Labor Day, won 110 games (an American League record), and won the pennant by 19 games. All the while, the focus of the nation was on Ruth's pursuit of his own record of 59 home runs in a season. This time, however, Ruth was not alone, as teammate Lou Gehrig proved capable of challenging the Babe for the crown. Gehrig and Ruth were tied with 24 home runs in late June, and the two were never more than two home runs apart through July and August. In early September, however, Ruth hit two home runs in the first game of a doubleheader at Fenway Park to take the lead permanently. He did not beat his record until the last game of the regular season, against the Washington Senators, when he hit his 60th homer in the 8th inning. He ended that season batting .356, drove in 164 runs, and slugged .772. The Yankees went on to sweep the Pittsburgh Pirates in the World Series.

Ruth in 1927

Gehrig, Tris Speaker, Ty Cobb, and Ruth

1928 proved to be an erratic season for the Yankees and for Ruth, who was plagued by early injuries and inconsistent play. The Philadelphia Athletics took over first place in early September, but the Yankees retook the lead later in September and won the pennant in the final weekend of the season. Ruth himself was on pace to eclipse 60 home runs before he went into a bit of a slump, and he finished with 54 home runs and a batting average of .323. The Yankees went on to sweep the Cardinals in the World Series, with Ruth batting .625 for the series and hitting three home runs in Game 4.

The 1929 season saw the Yankees adopt uniform numbers for the first time, with Ruth wearing #3. The team started off well, but they were eclipsed by the Philadelphia Athletics by the end of May, and the Yankees were never able to catch them. The team suffered a blow when Huggins died on September 25 of a bacterial skin infection. Ruth finished the season with a .345 batting average, 46 home runs, and 154 RBIs, but after the season, the Yankees hired Bob Shawkey as manager, bypassing Ruth himself after he had advocated for the job of player-manager. Ruppert and Barrow appear to never have seriously considered Ruth, sending the first hint that Ruth would have no future with the Yankees after his playing days were over.

Shawkey

Since Shawkey was a former Yankees player and teammate, Ruth never respected the new manager, and adding to the offseason stress, Ruth's contract was up for renegotiation. He rejected the Yankees initial offer of a one year contract at $70,000 (the same amount he had earned in his previous contract over three years), and instead he demanded a three year contract at $85,000 per year. When someone pointed out that this exceeded the pay of the president, Ruth commented, "Say, if I hadn't been sick last summer, I'd have broken hell out of that home run record! Besides, the President gets a four-year contract. I'm only asking for three." In the end, the Yankees and Ruth reached a compromise, and Ruth signed on for two years at $80,000 per year. It was an unprecedented amount, but the fact that the team was willing to play hardball with the sport's most prominent figure made clear that the slugger was nearing the end of his career.

The 1930 season proved to be one of Ruth's last productive seasons. He hit .359 with 49 homers and 153 RBIs, but the Athletics won their second pennant. The Yankees finished in third place, and at the end of the season, Cubs manager Joe McCarthy replaced Shawkey as manager. In 1931, Ruth's performance improved somewhat, as he hit .373 with 46 home runs and 163 RBIs, but the team missed out on the pennant again.

The 1932 season was a real turnaround for the Yankees. The team went 107-47 and won the pennant before facing the Cubs in the World Series. Ruth finished the regular season hitting .341 with 41 homers and 137 RBIs, but his performance in the first few games of the World Series was lackluster. The first two games in Yankee Stadium did not sell out, and Ruth merely hit two singles and was walked four times. In Chicago, the team was jeered at their hotel by hostile crowds, and at the ballpark some in the crowd threw lemons at Ruth. Ruth responded with a three run homer in the 1st inning, but by the 4th inning the game was tied 4-4. Hitting at the top of the fifth inning, the crowd and Cubs players yelled insults at Ruth, and with a 2-1 count, Ruth allegedly gestured in the direction of center field. After the next pitch, he pointed towards center field, then proceeded to hit the fifth pitch over the center field fence.

Over 85 years later, people still debate whether Ruth actually called his homer. There is footage of Ruth pointing, but it's hard to make out exactly what the context was. For his part, Ruth initially claimed, "Hell no, it isn't a fact. Only a damned fool would do a thing like that. You know there was a lot of pretty rough ribbing going on on both benches during that Series. When I swung and missed that first one, those Cubs really gave me a blast. So I grinned at 'em and held out one finger and told 'em it'd only take one to hit it. Then there was that second strike and they let me have it again. So I held up that finger again and I said I still had that one left. Naw, keed, you know damned well I wasn't pointin' anywhere. If I'd have done that, Root would have stuck the ball right in my ear. And besides that, I never knew anybody who could tell you ahead of time where he was going to hit a baseball. When I get to be that kind of fool, they`ll put me in the booby hatch."

Ruth would then subsequently claim he did call the shot, asserting, "My biggest home run thrill? The day I called that one on Root in the Yankee-Cub series. The whole crowd was riding me. I was riding 'em back with even rougher language. The Chicago bench was yelling 'Onya—onya—onya—you big yellow bum.' Root had thrown me two bad balls I didn't like. I protested both, then I pointed to the flag police in center field. I knew Root would feed me another just like the first two, so I moved up about eight inches closer and gave it the works. They tell me when they found that ball it was lopsided, shaped like an egg. I just got to thinking later what a terrible heel I'd have been that day if Root had struck me out, but I never thought of that till later. It's a good thing I didn't. What a mug I'd have been."

Ruth provided a far more descriptive – and almost certainly exaggerated – account of the called shot in his autobiography:

"No member of either team was sorer than I was. I had seen nothing my first time at bat that came close to looking good to me, and that only made me more determined to do something about taking the wind out of the sails of the Chicago players and their fans. I mean the fans who had spit on Claire [i.e., Ruth's wife].

"I came up in the fourth inning [sic] with Earle Combs on base ahead of me. My ears had been blistered so much before in my baseball career that I thought they had lost all feeling. But the blast that was turned on me by Cub players and some of the fans penetrated and cut deep. Some of the fans started throwing vegetables and fruit at me.

"I stepped back out of the box, then stepped in. And while Root was getting ready to throw his first pitch, I pointed to the bleachers which rise out of deep center field. Root threw one right across the gut of the plate and I let it go. But before the umpire could call it a strike - which it was - I raised my right hand, stuck out one finger and yelled, "Strike one!"

"The razzing was stepped up a notch.

"Root got set and threw again - another hard one through the middle. And once again I stepped back and held up my right hand and bawled, "Strike two!" It was.

"You should have heard those fans then. As for the Cub players they came out on the steps of their dugout and really let me have it.

"I guess the smart thing for Charlie to have done on his third pitch would have been to waste one.

"But he didn't, and for that I've sometimes thanked God.

"While he was making up his mind to pitch to me I stepped back again and pointed my finger at those bleachers, which only caused the mob to howl that much more at me.

"Root threw me a fast ball. If I had let it go, it would have been called a strike. But this was it. I swung from the ground with everything I had and as I hit the ball every muscle in my system, every sense I had, told me that I had never hit a better one, that as long as I lived nothing would ever feel as good as this.

"I didn't have to look. But I did. That ball just went on and on and on and hit far up in the center-field bleachers in exactly the spot I had pointed to.

"To me, it was the funniest, proudest moment I had ever had in baseball. I jogged down toward first base, rounded it, looked back at the Cub bench and suddenly got convulsed with laughter.

"You should have seen those Cubs. As Combs said later, 'There they were-all out on the top step and yelling their brains out - and then you connected and they watched it and then fell back as if they were being machine-gunned.'

"That home run-the most famous one I ever hit - did us some good. It was worth two runs, and we won that ball game, 7 to 5."

Bill Corum wrote in the *New York World Journal* that Ruth called his homer, making him one of two journalists to support the claim. Corum wrote, "Even people who were present at the game disagreed over what had happened. Words fail me. When he stood up there at the bat before 50,000 persons, calling the balls and the strikes with gestures for the benefit of the Cubs in their dugout, and then with two strikes on him, pointed out where he was going to hit the next one and hit it there, I gave up. That fellow is not human."

Conversely, Jim Gallagher was later quoted telling a far different version: "As for the booze-begotten yarn about Babe Ruth's 'called-shot,' I was there that day—at the elbow of Damon Runyon, no less, assigned to provide Runyon with any information he wanted about the Cubs or anyone else. No one in the press box or emergency press box that day, nobody at the press party that evening, and no one the next day even mentioned the incident except to emphasize the bitter exchange between the Cubs and Yankees. Charlie Root first laughed and, in his later years, grew angry when asked about it. One of the last letters I had from Dorothy Root before she died thanked me as a prophet of truth and the Babe himself, in Boston in 1935, said to me pretty much the same as your quote from Hal Totten."

As Ruth noted, the Yankees won Game 3, and the next day they won Game 4 to win the World Series.

The 1933 season proved to be Ruth's last productive season in baseball. He hit .301 to go with 34 home runs and 103 RBIs and 114 walks; but the Yankees finished in second place behind the Washington Senators. Connie Mack, managing the American League team in the first All-Star Game, selected Ruth to play right field. During the game, played at Chicago's Comiskey Park, he hit the first home run in an All-Star Game, leading the American League to a 4-2 win.

A 1933 card

The 1934 season was Ruth's last for the Yankees. By then, his binges off the field had taken their toll, rendering him almost entirely unable to run or field. He accepted a one year contact at $35,000. In the twilight of his career, he hit .288 and 22 home runs, and was selected to the All-Star team. With that, Ruth's full-time playing days were over.

The End

Seemingly finished as a player, Ruth nevertheless wanted to stay in baseball as a manager. Before the 1934 season, Ruppert offered to make Ruth the manager of the minor-league Newark

Bears, but Ruth turned the job down on the advice of his wife and his business manager. The owner of the Detroit Tigers offered to name Ruth player-manager if the Yankees traded him to the team. Ruth negotiated over the phone with Navin from Hawaii (he was there for a celebrity golf tournament), but when Navin refused to give Ruth a portion of the Tigers' box office receipts, the talks ended.

There were few other teams interested in Ruth as manager, as the *Washington Evening Star* reported: "It has become increasingly evident, If not absolutely definite, that there is no opportunity In the American League for Babe Ruth to fulfill his ambition to launch a managerial career next season. What will happen after 1935, when Joe McCarthy's contract runs out with the Yankees, and perhaps other vacancies develop, remains to be seen. Meanwhile the Babe is in the position of having burned his bridges behind him, with no place to go after he finishes a trip around the world. He had publicly declared himself out of the player ranks, which makes it official, but it is difficult to imagine his retirement, even if there isn't a manager s job available. Besides, the great man can always change his mind. In rapid succession within the past fortnight the possibility of Ruth becoming manager of the Philadelphia, Boston or Washington club In the American League has been discussed and discarded. It is no secret that most major league magnates consider the Babe too big a gamble, as a manager, to justify the substantial investment required in signing him up. 'Ruth unquestionably has the background, the personality and many of the qualifications essential to becoming a successful major league manager,' one club owner explained recently. 'There should be a spot where he could have a chance to show what he can do with a ball club but, frankly, I don't know anybody willing to undertake the experiment. The big question concerns Ruth's ability to maintain discipline. He has never had such responsibility. It is also doubtful whether he would take the time and exhibit patience necessary to building up a second division club. Meanwhile the more successful teams do not need him."

While Ruth was on a barnstorming tour with his wife, Ruppert negotiated with Boston Braves owner Judge Emil Fuchs. Fuchs was interested in Ruth's ability to attract crowds to the ballpark; the National League team had finished fourth in both 1933 and 1934, but it drew poorly at the box office. After a series of meetings, the Yankees traded Ruth to the Braves on February 26, 1935, but not as a full-time player. He would play part-time, become a team vice-president, and would be made assistant manager. In private, Fuchs promised Ruth a share of the profits, the possibility of becoming a co-owner, and even becoming team manager as early as 1936. It was, in Ruppert's terms, "the greatest opportunity Ruth ever had."

Fuchs

Ruth's new career with only the third Major League team he had played for began auspiciously enough. He hit a homer in leading the Braves to a 4-2 win over the New York Giants before an Opening Day crowd of 25,000 in Boston, and he had two hits in the second game of the season. After that, however, things quickly went downhill. His age and poor physical shape were clear for all to see, and Ruth performed poorly on those few occasions he even played. By the middle of May, his condition was so bad that he could barely trot around the bases on those rare occasions he hit the ball. He made so many errors during games that at one point the three Braves pitchers told the team manager Bill McKechnie that they would not play if Ruth was in the lineup. In addition to his poor performance, he clashed with the McKenchie, mostly because Ruth felt the manager would not take his advice. It also became clear to Ruth that Fuchs had no intention of making him manager, and his only job as vice president, he later claimed, was to sign autographs and make public appearances. As far as becoming a part-owner, that proved false as well, Fuchs actually wanted Ruth to invest in the team.

The decline in Ruth's abilities as a player was evident to everyone, even as Ruth denied any intention of retiring. The *Washington Evening Star* reported on May 17, 1935 that Ruth "somewhat angrily denied published reports that he was 'all washed up' and intended to quit as a player on completion of the Boston Braves' swing through the West, starting today in St. Louis." The article went on to tell readers, "Two and one-half months ago, when the Babe cast his lot with the Braves in the triple capacity of player, vice president and assistant to Manager Bill McKechnie—the three jobs generally figured to aggregate $40,000 for the season—he was regarded as the solution for the club's financial ailments. Since then baseball men have speculated on the possibility of a midseason shift by which Ruth would become field manager and McKechnie elevated to the job of general manager Ruth's ambition for two years has been to manage a big league club Whether he will be given his first chance in Boston depends on the ability of President Fuchs to meet financial obligations within the next two months, retain control of the club and make the double managerial shift. This failing, the Babe in all probability will seek a post elsewhere. 'I am not ready to write finis to my career as an active player,' said Ruth."

In fact, the story was true. Ruth had decided by early May that his playing days were over, and he had approached Fuchs about retiring on May 12. Fuchs persuaded Ruth to remain at least until after the Memorial Day doubleheader in Philadelphia, after the western road trip. He performed poorly, and his batting average sank to .155 with only two more home runs for the season. He hit his last home run on May 25 in a game against Pittsburgh, offering a glimpse of the Babe Ruth of old. Sailing over the right field upper deck, it was the first home run ever completely out of Forbes Field. Paul Waner, one of the Pirates, said admiringly, "Who said the old Babe can't smack 'em any more? That second homer must have traveled 450 feet and the third came close to 600 if I'm not mistaken." The great Honus Wagner, managing the Pirates at the time, said, "I've seen some great hitters and long distance hits in my day, but none like the Babe's on Saturday. He's the greatest home run hitter of all time."

The first game of the doubleheader in Philadelphia was Ruth's last. He officially retired on June 2, finishing the season with a .181 batting average and six home runs. He had finished his career with 714 homers, a mark that would only be eclipsed by Hank Aaron nearly 40 years later.

With the headline "Unwanted, Ruth Admits he is Through; Babe's Fadeout Held Complete," the *Washington Evening Star* reported, "A seething mountain of a man was George Herman Ruth today, but all the arguments in the world, all the hot words, bitter recriminations that have passed between him and the Boston Braves couldn't hide this epochal line for baseball's history: Babe Ruth is all done. His final turbulent exchange with Emil Fuchs, president of the Braves, and Bill McKechnie, manager of the club, served today only to emphasize the completeness of the passing of the man who for 21 straight years has been making major league history. The Babe admits he's through as a ball player, and it's hardly likely a single club in either major league would chance the grief that followed Ruth to Boston, even though he did bring swollen gate receipts along with it."

In retirement, Ruth played golf and in several exhibition baseball games, but no team expressed an interest in hiring him as a manager, despite Ruth's continued desire to hold such a position. Team owners cited Ruth's flamboyant lifestyle as an impediment to being considered as a manager. He still continued to draw crowds, however, and this led the Brooklyn Dodgers to hire him in 1938 as a first base coach. It was made clear to Ruth from the outset by the team's general manager Larry MacPhall that Ruth was not under consideration for the manager's job when the current team manager retired at the end of the season. It was another situation where

Ruth had been hired for his celebrity rather than his baseball prowess, as he was not called upon to relay signs and instead was expected to appear on the field in uniform and encourage players. Due to his inability to get along with team captain Leo Durocher, hired as team manager at the end of the season, Ruth left his job as first base coach. He would never work in any capacity in baseball again.

Ruth continued to make public appearances, drawing crowds who remembered the legend during his glory days. On July 4, 1939, Ruth appeared with the other members of the 1927 New York Yankees at Lou Gehrig Appreciation day to honor his former teammate, who was forced into early retirement by Amyotrophic lateral sclerosis. Ruth dramatically hugged the dying man, but their relationship had become frigid over the years; *The New York Times* noted, "The last straw came when Ruth spoke disparagingly of Gehrig's cherished consecutive game streak. He said he regarded it as little more than a boring statistic. 'This Iron Horse stuff is just a lot of baloney,' Ruth growled. 'I think he's making one of the worst mistakes a player can make. He ought to learn to sit on the bench and rest. They're not going to pay off on how many games he's played in a row.'" In fact, after that commemoration, Ruth ignored Gehrig during the last two years of the stricken man's life, and the *New York Times* described Ruth's behavior at Gehrig's funeral: "'Lou's father and mother were there when we came to the house,' wrote songwriter Fred Fisher, a good friend of the Gehrigs, to a doctor who had cared for Lou during his last fight against amyotrophic lateral sclerosis. 'There were a lot of friends there, too. Eleanor was very composed, having been prepared for the shock. But she became very angry when Ruth and his wife came in very intoxicated. He certainly wasn't wanted by the Gehrigs, as there was friction between them for years.'"

In 1936, Ruth became one of the first five players elected to the Hall of Fame in Cooperstown, New York, and in July 1939 he attended the opening of the Hall. As radio broadcasts of games became more popular, Ruth sought a job as a broadcaster, thinking his celebrity and baseball knowledge would ensure large audiences, but he received no offers.

As many celebrities in America did, Ruth lent his fame to the war effort during World War II. He made many personal appearances, including his last appearance as a baseball player at Yankee Stadium in 1943. During an exhibition for the Army-Navy Relief fund, Ruth hit a long fly ball off of Walter Johnson, and though it was clearly a foul ball, Ruth, ever the showman, circled the bases anyway.

In 1946, Ruth's years of drinking and poor health really began to take its toll. In November of that year, he entered French Hospital in New York complaining of severe pain over his left eye and difficulty swallowing. Tests revealed he had an inoperable tumor at the base of his skull and neck, known as nasopharyngeal carcinoma. The doctors, on the advice of his family, did not tell him he had cancer because of fears that he might harm himself.

Thanks to his fame, Ruth had access to the latest experimental treatments, including the first use of drugs and radiation simultaneously. He was discharged from the hospital in February and went to Florida to recuperate. Baseball Commissioner Happy Chandler proclaimed April 27 Babe Ruth Day around the leagues. At Yankee Stadium, former teammates and others spoke in honor of Ruth.

Ruth said a few words as well:

> "Thank you very much, ladies and gentlemen.

> "You know how bad my voice sounds -- well it feels just as bad.

> "You know this baseball game of ours comes up from the youth. That means the boys.

> "And after you're a boy and grow up to know how to play ball, then you come to the boys you see representing themselves today in your national pastime, the only real game -- I think -- in the world, baseball.

> "As a rule, some people think if you give them a football, or a baseball, or something like that -- naturally they're athletes right away.

> "But you can't do that in baseball.

> "You've gotta start from way down [at] the bottom, when you're six or seven years of age. You can't wait until you're fifteen or sixteen. You gotta let it grow up with you. And if you're successful, and you try hard enough, you're bound to come out on top -- just like these boys have come to the top now.

> "There's been so many lovely things said about me, and I'm glad that I've had the opportunity to thank everybody.

> "Thank you."

Chemotherapy provided some hope for Ruth. who showed dramatic improvement during the summer of 1947, so much so that he was able to go on a national promotional tour for the Ford Motor Company on behalf of American Legion baseball. He appeared again at Yankee Stadium in September for an old-timers game, but he was not well enough to pitch.

Later in the year, however, Ruth weakened as the treatments failed to make any real headway against the cancer. He was too weak to help with the writing of his autobiography, *The Babe Ruth Story.* In and out of the hospital, he took one last trip to Florida in February 1948 before returning to New York in mid-March for a book signing party. He also traveled to California to watch the filming of the movie based on his autobiography.

On June 5, 1948, Ruth visited Yale University to donate the manuscript of his book to the Yale Library. There, he met with the Yale Baseball team and shook hands with the team captain, who was none other than George H.W. Bush.

On June 13, Ruth visited Yankee Stadium one final time to celebrate the 25th anniversary of "The House that Ruth Built". He was gaunt and thin, and he had such difficulty talking that he had to use a bat as a cane as he stood with some of his old teammates from the 1923 team.

After a final trip on behalf of American Legion Baseball, Ruth entered Memorial Hospital. He was able to leave the hospital for short trips, including one final visit to his native Baltimore.

On July 26, 1948, he appeared at the premiere of the film *The Babe Ruth Story*, but his condition gradually grew worse, leaving him unable to speak.

One of the few visitors allowed to see him in his final days was National League President and future Baseball Commissioner Ford Frick. Frick recalled, "It was a terrible moment. Ruth was so thin it was unbelievable. He had been such a big man and his arms were just skinny little bones, and his face was so haggard" When I came in he lifted his eyes toward me and raised his right arm a little, only about three or four inches off the bed, and then it fell back again. I went over to the bed and I said, 'Babe, Paul Carey said you wanted to see me.' And Ruth said, in that terrible voice, 'Ford, I always wanted to see you.' It was just a polite thing to say. I stayed a few minutes and left and I spoke to Claire against across the hall and then I went home and the next day he was dead."

Ruth died in his sleep on August 16, 1948 at the age of 53. In its obituary for the baseball legend, *Time* magazine summarized his colorful career:

> "He was unforgettable, even when he struck out. His swing whirled him around until his slender legs were twisted beneath him. And the times when his big bat did connect were baseball's biggest moments. The spell lasted until the Babe had trotted around the base paths, taking mincing steps on his small feet, tipping his cap to the mighty, reverent roar from the stands.

> "Sportwriters knocked themselves out thinking up new names and superlatives for him: The Sultan of Swat, the Bambino, The Colossus of Clout. He didn't need all that; he was color itself—a fellow built on heroic, swaggering lines, an enormous head on a barrel of a body.

> "In the golden '20s, the years of the big names—the years of Dempsey, Tilden and Bobby Jones—Babe Ruth was the biggest draw of them all. With his big bat, he put baseball back on its feet and back in the hearts of the fans after the 1919 'Black Sox' scandal.

"He began his big-league career as a crack southpaw pitcher for the Boston Red Sox. But he was also a slugger without peer, and when he clouted most of his record 714 home runs, he wore a New York Yankee uniform, played the outfield. Son of a Baltimore saloonkeeper, he was brought up in a Baltimore school for delinquents, and he never quite grew up. In his first years in baseball, he scoffed at training rules, took his drinks where he found them, abused umpires, once chased up into the stands after an abusive fan.

"His emotions were always out on the surface, which was one reason all the fans thought they knew and understood him. Even when the late Jimmy Walker gave him a talking-to before a banquet, the Babe gulped, and with enormous tears rolling down his enormous face, promised the kids of America he would reform. He tried to. But nothing could stop him from living handsomely.

"He made more than $2,000,000 and spent most of it. He once confessed: 'I lost $35,000 on one horse race alone.' Ban Johnson, late president of the American League once said with asperity but accuracy: 'Ruth has the mind of a 15-year-old boy.' The Babe couldn't even remember the names of his teammates. He greeted everybody, old or young, with his famed welcome: 'Hello kid.'"

Babe Ruth's open casket laid in state in the rotunda of Yankee Stadium for two days, with an estimated 77,000 people filing past to pay respects. A crowd of 75,000 stood outside of St. Patrick's Cathedral during his funeral mass before he was buried at Gate of Heaven cemetery in Hawthorne, New York. Cardinal Francis Spellman wrote the epitaph that appears on the headstone: "May the divine spirit that animated Babe Ruth to win the crucial game of life inspire the youth of America."

Decades after Ruth's death, Stephen Lang, who played Ruth in a biopic about the sports legend's life, summed up Ruth's legacy succinctly but profoundly: "Ruth personified an entire period, the Roaring '20s, which personified America. Nobody roared louder than Ruth."

Online Resources

Other books about sports by Charles River Editors

Other books about Babe Ruth on Amazon

Further Reading

Appel, Marty (2012). Pinstripe Empire: The New York Yankees From Before the Babe to After the Boss. New York: Bloombury USA. ISBN 978-1-60819-492-6.

Creamer, Robert W. (1992) [1974]. Babe: The Legend Comes to Life (First Fireside ed.). New York: Simon & Schuster. ISBN 978-0-671-76070-0.

Graham, Frank (1943). The New York Yankees: An Informal History. New York: G.P. Putnam's Sons. OCLC 1825210.

Hoyt, Waite (1948). Babe Ruth As I Knew Him. New York: Dell Publishing.

James, Bill (2003) [2001]. The New Bill James Historical Baseball Abstract (First Free Press trade paperback ed.). New York: Free Press. ISBN 978-0-7432-2722-3.

Leavy, Jane (2018). The Big Fella: Babe Ruth and the World He Created. Harper. Montville, Leigh (2006). The Big Bam: The Life and Times of Babe Ruth. New York: Broadway Books. ISBN 978-0-7679-1971-5.

Meany, Tom (1947). Babe Ruth: The Big Moments of the Big Fella. New York: A.S. Barnes.

Neyer, Rob (2000). Rob Neyer's Big Book of Baseball Blunders. New York: Fireside Books. ISBN 978-0-7432-8491-2.

Pietrusza, David (1998). Judge and Jury: The Life and Times of Judge Kenesaw Mountain Landis. South Bend, Indiana: Diamond Communications. ISBN 978-1-888698-09-1.

Reisler, Jim (2004). Babe Ruth: Launching the Legend. New York: McGraw-Hill. ISBN 978-0-07-143244-3.

Ruth, Babe; Considine, Tom (1948). The Babe Ruth Story. New York: E.P. Dutton.

Ruth, Babe; Cobb, William R. (2011). Playing the Game: My Early Years in Baseball. Minneola, NY: Dover Publications.

Sherman, Ed (2014). Babe Ruth's Called Shot: The Myth and Mystery of Baseball's Greatest Home Run. Guilford, Connecticut: Lyons Press. ISBN 978-0-7627-8539-1.

Smelser, Marshall (1975). The Life That Ruth Built. New York: Quadrangle/New York Times Book Co. ISBN 978-0-8129-0540-3.

Spatz, Lyle; Steinberg, Lyle (2010). 1921: The Yankees, The Giants, & The Battle For Baseball Supremacy in New York. Lincoln, Nebraska: University of Nebraska Press. ISBN 978-0-8032-3999-9.

Stout, Glenn (2016). The Selling of the Babe: The Deal That Changed Baseball and Created a Legend. Thomas Dunne Books. ISBN 1250064317.

Stout, Glenn (2002). Yankee Century: 100 Years of New York Yankees Baseball. New York: Houghton Mifflin Company. ISBN 978-0-618-08527-9.

Wagenheim, Kal (1974). Babe Ruth: His Life and Legend. New York: Praeger Publishers. ISBN 978-0-275-19980-7.

Free Books by Charles River Editors

We have brand new titles available for free most days of the week. To see which of our titles are currently free, click on this link.

Discounted Books by Charles River Editors

We have titles at a discount price of just 99 cents everyday. To see which of our titles are currently 99 cents, click on this link.

Made in the USA
Las Vegas, NV
23 February 2021